Knit your own
BOYFRIEND

KNIT 2 TOG
4EVA

Knit your own
BOYFRIEND

by Carol Meldrum

Contents

THE PERFECT BOYFRIEND ON KNITTING

'I did this scene in a movie where I was in a room
full of old ladies who were knitting, and it was
an all-day scene, so they showed me how. It was
one of the most relaxing days of my life. If I had
to design my perfect day, that would be it. And
you get something out of it at the end. You get
a nice present. For someone who wants an oddly
shaped, off-putting scarf.'

Ryan Gosling

Basic Doll

You can use this pattern to make four different doll shapes: short and slim; short and stocky; tall and slim; tall and stocky.

Height

Short doll: 27cm (10¾in)
Tall doll: 30cm (12in)

Materials

DK-weight yarn in skin colour of your choice (see right)
Pair of 3.25mm (US 3) knitting needles
Polyester toy stuffing
Tapestry and embroidery needles
Embroidery thread for eyes and mouth

Tension

Approx 24 sts and 32 rows to 10cm (4in) over stocking stitch using 3.25mm (US 3) needles

Skin colours

The boyfriend dolls can be made using any skin colour you like. The yarn used for the skin is referred to as 'yarn A' in each of the doll patterns, so it is easy to substitute a different colour from the one shown if you wish. The following colours have been used in this book:
Rowan Cotton Glacé (100% cotton; approx 115m/125yds per 50g ball):
White skin: 725 Ecru (such as Artist, page 38)
Pale beige/pinkish skin: 730 Oyster (such as Sports Star, page 52)
Dark brown skin: 843 Toffee (such as Spaceman, page 60)
Rowan Pure Wool DK (100% super wash wool; approx 130m/142yds per 50g ball):
Light brown skin: 054 Tan (such as Surfer Dude, page 35)

These instructions are for making a naked doll. Some of the boyfriends have clothing worked as part of the basic doll by changing yarn colours. The instructions for each boyfriend specify where to change colour.

Short and stocky doll   Short and slim doll

Pattern

Legs and feet

Cast on 32 sts.

Starting with a knit row, work 6 rows in stocking stitch.

Row 7 (RS): K14, k2tog, k2togtbl, knit to end. (30 sts)

Row 8: P15, turn; slip remaining sts onto spare needle or stitch holder.

Work on 15 sts only to make the left leg, working 30 rows in stocking stitch for a short doll or 36 rows for a tall doll.

Shape left foot

Row 1 (RS): K3, m1, k1, m1, knit to end. (17 sts)

Row 2: Purl.

Row 3: K4, m1, k1, m1, knit to end. (19 sts)

Row 4: Purl.

Next row: K5, m1, k1, m1, k5, turn; do not work remaining sts on the left-hand needle.

Next row: Slip 1, p11, turn.

Next row: Slip 1, k4, m1, k1, m1, k4, turn.

Next row: Slip 1, p9, turn.

Next row: Slip 1, k3, m1, k1, m1, k3, turn.

Next row: Slip 1, p7, turn.

Next row: Slip 1, knit to end. Cast off.

With RS facing, rejoin yarn to 15 sts on spare needle or stitch holder and work to match other leg.

Shape right foot

Row 1 (RS): K11, m1, k1, m1, knit to end. (17 sts)

Row 2: Purl.

Row 3: K12, m1, k1, m1, knit to end. (19 sts)

Row 4: Purl.

Next row: K13, m1, k1, m1, k4, turn; do not work remaining sts on the left-hand needle.

Next row: Slip 1, p10, turn.

Next row: Slip 1, k4, m1, k1, m1, k4, turn.

Next row: Slip 1, p9, turn.

Next row: Slip 1, k3, m1, k1, m1, k3, turn.

Next row: Slip 1, p8, turn.

Next row: Slip 1, knit to end. Cast off.

Short and slim doll

Body and head

With RS facing, pick up and knit 32 sts along cast-on edge of legs.

Row 1 (WS): Purl.

Row 2 (RS): K7, m1, k2, m1, k14, m1, k2, m1, k7. (36 sts)

Slim body shape only:

Starting and ending with a purl row, work 11 rows in stocking stitch for a short doll or 15 rows for a tall doll.

Row 14(18): K8, m1, k2, m1, k16, m1, k2, m1, k8. (40 sts)

Starting and ending with a purl row, work 5 rows in stocking stitch for a short doll or 7 rows for a tall doll.

Stocky body shape only:

Row 3: Purl.

Row 4: K8, m1, k2, m1, k16, m1, k2, m1, k8. (40 sts)

Row 5: Purl.

Row 6: K9, m1, k2, m1, k18, m1, k2, m1, k9. (44 sts)

Starting and ending with a purl row, work 9 rows in stocking stitch for a short doll or 11 rows for a tall doll.

Row 16(18): K8, k2tog, k2, k2togtbl, k16, k2tog, k2, k2togtbl, k8. (40 sts)

Starting and ending with a purl row, work 3 rows in stocking stitch for a short doll or 7 rows for a tall doll.

All dolls:

Row 20(26): K7, k2tog, k2, k2togtbl, k14, k2tog, k2, k2togtbl, k7. (36 sts)

Row 21(27): Purl.

Row 22(28): K6, k2togtbl, k2, k2tog, k12, k2togtbl, k2, k2tog, k6. (32 sts)

Row 23(29): Purl.

Row 24(30): K5, k2tog, k2, k2togtbl, k10, k2tog, k2, k2togtbl, k5. (28 sts)

Row 25(31): P4, p2togtbl, p2, p2tog, p8, p2togtbl, p2, p2tog, p4. (24 sts)

Row 26(32): K3, k2tog, k2, k3togtbl, k4, k3tog, k2, k2togtbl, k3. (18 sts)

Neck and head

Starting and ending with a purl row, work 3 rows in stocking stitch.

Start shaping head as follows:

Row 1 (RS): K4, m1, k2, m1, k6, m1, k2, m1, k4. (22 sts)

Row 2: P5, m1, p2, m1, p8, m1, p2, m1, p5. (26 sts)

Row 3: K6, m1, k2, m1, k10, m1, k2, m1, k6. (30 sts)

Starting and ending with a purl row, work 11 rows in stocking stitch.

Row 15: K5, k2tog, k2, k2togtbl, k8, k2tog, k2, k2togtbl, k5. (26 sts)

Row 16: P4, p2togtbl, p2, p2tog, p6, p2togtbl, p2, p2tog, p4. (22 sts)

Row 17: K3, k2tog, k2, k2togtbl, k4, k2tog, k2, k2togtbl, k3. (18 sts)

Break off yarn and thread through stitches on needle, but do not pull tight.

Arm and hand (make 2)

Cast on 12 sts.

Starting with a knit row, work 26 rows in stocking stitch for a short doll or 30 rows for a tall doll.

Shape hand

Next row (RS): K1, [k2tog] twice, k2, [k2tog] twice, k1. (8 sts)

Next row: Purl.
Next row: K2, [m1, k2] to end. (11 sts)
Next row: Purl.
Next row: K2, m1, k3, m1, k4, m1, k2.
(14 sts)
Starting and ending with a purl row, work
5 rows in stocking stitch.
Next row: K1, [k2tog] to last st, k1. (8 sts)
Break off yarn and thread through
stitches on needle. Pull tight and secure
the end.

Sole of foot (make 2)

Cast on 3 sts.
Row 1: Knit.
Row 2: K1, m1, k1, m1, k1. (5 sts)
Knit 13 rows.
Row 16: K2tog, k1, k2tog. (3 sts)
Row 17: Knit.
Cast off.

Finishing

Use the pictures as a guide throughout
the finishing of all pieces. Sew seams
using mattress stitch or whip stitch (pages
72-73), and use matching yarn unless
stated otherwise. Weave in all loose ends,
using seams where appropriate, and
block and press pieces if required. When
inserting stuffing, use a chopstick or
similar tool to help push it right down into
hands and feet. You can sculpt the doll's
body shape by varying the quantity of
stuffing and how you position it, but take
care not to overstuff.

Legs and feet

Sew side edges of each leg and foot
together to form inner leg seams. Sew
back seam on doll's bottom, then sew
soles to base of feet. Insert stuffing into
legs and feet.

Body and head

Sew back seam on body, then insert
stuffing down through head. Sew back
seam on head, then insert stuffing. Pull
thread at top of head tight and secure
with a few stitches.
To define neck, thread tapestry needle
with length of yarn but do not secure or
tie knot. Insert needle at back seam just
under first row of increasing for head.
Weave in and out of stitches around neck.
Pull tight and tie a double knot, then sew
in loose ends.

Arms

Sew side edges of each arm together to
form underarm seams. Insert stuffing,
then sew up the top opening. Sew arms to
body, using shaping marks on shoulders
to position them symmetrically.

Hair and face

Hair: Choose a hairstyle (page 14) and sew
it on to the doll's head.
Eyes: Work French knots (page 73), using
embroidery thread wrapped around
needle 5 times (any colour you like).
Mouth: Work in backstitch (page 73) using
red embroidery thread.
Facial hair: Add facial hair if desired
(page 19).

Hairstyles

Here are 10 hairstyles to choose from, plus some facial hair.

Materials

Yarn in colour of your choice; DK-weight yarn is used unless stated otherwise, but you can vary the yarn weight to achieve finer or thicker hair as desired
Pair of 3.25mm (US 3) knitting needles
Tapestry needle
Crochet hook for ponytail and slicked-back hairstyles
Embroidery needle and thread for stubble

Short hairstyles

Short back and sides

Cast on 9 sts.
Row 1 (WS): Purl.
Row 2 (RS): K1, m1, knit to last st, m1, k1. (11 sts)
Row 3: P1, m1, purl to last st, m1, p1. (13 sts)
Row 4: Knit.
Row 5: Purl.
Row 6: As row 2. (15 sts)
Row 7: As row 3. (17 sts)
Row 8: Cast on 2 sts, knit to end. (19 sts)
Row 9: Cast on 2 sts, purl to end. (21 sts)
Row 10: Knit.
Row 11: Purl.
Row 12: K2, [k2togtbl, k3] 3 times, k2togtbl, k2. (17 sts)
Row 13: Purl.
Row 14: K1, [k2togtbl, k2] to end. (13 sts)
Row 15: Purl.
Row 16: K1, [k2togtbl, k1] to end. (9 sts)
Knit 4 rows.
Cast off.
Pin and stitch hair to doll's head, with cast-off edge towards top of head.

Side parting

Cast on 9 sts and work rows 1-7 as for short back and sides hairstyle.

Row 8 (RS): Cast on 3 sts, knit to end. (20 sts)

Row 9: Cast on 4 sts, purl to end. (24 sts)

Row 10: Knit.

Row 11: As row 9. (28 sts)

Row 12: K1, [k2togtbl, k2] 6 times, k2togtbl, k1. (21 sts)

Row 13: Purl.

Row 14: K1, [k2togtbl, k1] twice, k2togtbl, k3, [k2tog, k1] 3 times. (15 sts)

Row 15: P1, [p2tog] 3 times, p1, [p2togtbl] 3 times, p1. (9 sts)

Break off yarn and thread through stitches on needle. Pull tight and secure the end.

Pin and stitch hair to doll's head, with cast-off edge towards top of head.

Afro

Using Aran-weight yarn, cast on 4 sts. Knit 10 rows.

Row 11: K1, m1, k2, m1, k1. (6 sts)

Continue knitting every row until strip fits from top of head to back neck. Cast off.

Pin and stitch hair to doll's head, with cast-off edge towards top of head.

Work a few French knots around hairline (yarn wrapped around needle 3 times).

Slicked back

Curly

Side parting

1950s quiff

Cast on 13 sts.

Starting with a knit row, work 4 rows in stocking stitch.

Row 5 (RS): K1, m1, knit to last st, m1, k1. (15 sts)

Row 6: Purl.

Repeat last 2 rows five times more. (25 sts)

Row 17: K1, m1, knit to end. (26 sts)

Row 18: Purl.

Repeat last 2 rows once more. (27 sts)

Row 21: [K4, k2tog] twice, k3, [k2tog, k4] twice. (23 sts)

Row 22: Purl.

Row 23: K3, [k2tog, k3] to end. (19 sts)

Row 24: Purl.

Row 25: K3, [k2tog, k2] to end. (15 sts)

Row 26: Purl.

Row 27: K2, [k2tog, k1] to last st, k1. (11 sts)

Break off yarn and thread through stitches on needle. Pull tight and secure the end.

Pin and stitch hair to doll's head, with cast-off edge towards top of head.

Wrap a length of yarn around a couple of fingers, then place it on top front of head and stitch into place to produce a neat quiff or messed-up bed-head look.

Bald

Take the easy option and make yourself a bald boyfriend. Probably best not to add a comb-over...

Stubble

Neat 1950s quiff

Shoulder length, moustache and sideburns

Long hairstyles

Hair base

All of the long hairstyles are built onto a hair base worked as follows:

Using yarn weight specified for your chosen hairstyle, cast on 9 sts.

Row 1 (WS): Purl.

Row 2 (RS): K1, m1, knit to last st, m1, k1. (11 sts)

Row 3: Purl.

Repeat last 2 rows three times more. (17 sts)

Row 10: Knit.

Row 11: Purl.

Row 12: As row 2. (19 sts)

Row 13: P1, m1, purl to last st, m1, p1. (21 sts)

Row 14: K2, [k2togtbl, k3] 3 times, k2togtbl, k2. (17 sts)

Row 15: Purl.

Row 16: K1, [k2togtbl, k2] to end. (13 sts)

Row 17: Purl.

Row 18: K1, [k2togtbl, k1] to end. (9 sts)

Row 19: P1, p2tog, p3, p2togtbl, p1. (7 sts)

Row 20: K1, k2togtbl, k1, k2tog, k1. (5 sts)

Cast off.

Pin and stitch hair base to doll's head, with cast-off edge towards top of head, then continue as described below.

Curly

Special abbreviation: L1 = loop 1: insert RH needle into stitch as if to knit, wrap yarn over and around RH needle point and forefinger twice, then over and around RH needle point once more; draw all 3 loops through st and slip onto LH needle, then insert RH needle through back of these 3 loops and original st and ktogtbl.

Cast on 9 sts.

Row 1 (RS): Knit.

Row 2: K1, m1, knit to last st, m1, k1. (11 sts)

Row 3: As row 2. (13 sts)

Knit 2 rows.

Row 6: As row 2. (15 sts)

Row 7: L1, m1, [L1, k1] 6 times, L1, m1, L1. (17 sts)

Row 8: Cast on 2 sts, knit to end. (19 sts)

Row 9: Cast on 2 sts, [k1, L1] to last st, k1. (21 sts)

Row 10: Knit.

Row 11: L1, [k1, L1] to end.

Row 12: K2, [k2togtbl, k3] 3 times, k2togtbl, k2. (17 sts)

Row 13: K1, [L1, k1] to end.

Row 14: K1, [k2togtbl, k2] to end. (13 sts)

Row 15: As row 11.

Row 16: K1, [k2togtbl, k1] to end. (9 sts)

Row 17: As row 13.

Row 18: Knit.

Cast off.

Pin and stitch hair to doll's head, with cast-off edge towards top of head.

Ponytail

Using Aran-weight yarn for both hair base and ponytail, cut 30cm (12in) lengths of yarn and divide into nine sections of 2-3 strands.

Attach the strands along top front seam of hair base by inserting a crochet hook under a stitch, folding a section of hair in half and pulling it through to form a loop, then pass the cut ends of the strands through the loop and pull tight to form a tassel.

Gather into a bunch at back of head and use a length of yarn to tie into a ponytail. Trim the ponytail if you want it shorter.

Slicked back

Cut 8cm (3¼in) lengths of yarn and divide into nine sections of 2 strands.
Attach the strands to the hair base as for a ponytail.

Slick the strands back over the hair base and work a few stitches at back of head to secure.

Shoulder length

Cut thirty 15cm (6in) lengths of yarn. Lay the strands across the hair base and pin in place. Using matching yarn, work backstitch from top of head to neckline to secure strands and create centre parting.

Dreadlocks

Use 4ply yarn for the hair base and for sewing the dreadlocks to it.

Using super chunky yarn, cut nine 14cm (5¹/₂in) lengths for bottom layer of dreadlocks and twelve 18cm (7in) lengths for top layer. Fold each strand in half. Thread tapestry needle with 4ply yarn. Inserting needle through fold of yarn, thread all of the shorter dreadlocks onto the needle. Slide the strands together so that the layer is 9cm (3¹/₂in) wide. Pin the

Dreadlocks

Short back and sides

18

layer around head, approx 4cm (1¹/₂in) from centre top, and stitch into position. Thread all of the longer dreadlocks together as before, slide together so that the top layer is 10cm (4in) wide and then tie the 4ply yarn to form a loop. Fold the loop in half, pin along top of head in a slightly off-centre diagonal and stitch into position.

Facial hair

Goatee
Cast on 5 sts.
Row 1: Purl.
Row 2: K1, k3tog, k1. (3 sts)
Row 3: Purl.
Row 4: K3tog.
Fasten off.
Pin and stitch onto doll's face just under mouth.

Stubble
Using embroidery thread, work French knots around mouth and jaw (wrapped around needle 3 times).

Moustache
Cast on 11 sts.
Row 1: K1, slip 1, k2tog, psso, k3, k3tog, k1. (7 sts)
Cast off 1 st, k3tog, pass cast-off st over k3tog just worked, cast off remaining stitches.
Pin and stitch onto doll's face just above mouth.

Sideburns (make 2)
Cast on 5 sts.
Row 1: Cast off 2 sts, knit to end.
Cast off remaining sts.
Pin and stitch onto doll's face, making sure that they are positioned symmetrically.

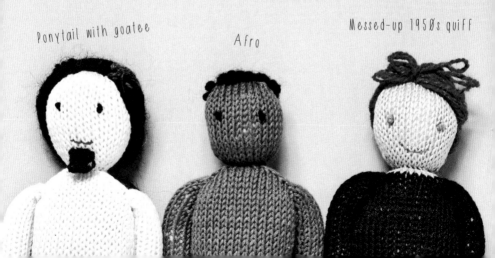

Ponytail with goatee

Afro

Messed-up 1950s quiff

T-shirt and Jeans

The classic combo that most boys never grow out of wearing.

Materials

Old T-shirt or 20cm (8in) square of jersey fabric

Old jeans or 25cm (10in) square of denim fabric (or use another fabric for a different look)

Sharp sewing needle

Thread to match T-shirt fabric, plus white and orange for jeans

Instructions

Jeans

Using template on page 75, cut out front and back of trousers from denim fabric. If you want your jeans to have a turn-up, add an extra 1-1.5cm (^{3}/$_8$-^{5}/$_8$in) at the bottom. Using 5mm (^{1}/$_4$in) seam allowance and backstitch, pin the pieces RS together and sew side seams and then inner leg seams. Turn RS out.

Waistband

Cut a 3cm (1^1/$_4$in) wide strip of denim long enough to go around top of trousers with a 1cm (^{3}/$_8$in) overlap at front. Fold the fabric lengthways into three sections, like an envelope. Using orange thread, sew a line of running stitch slightly in from top and bottom folds.

If using old jeans, cut the waistband from the bottom hem to utilize the contrast stitching.

Pin waistband around top of trousers, starting at centre front and allowing the other end to overlap. If using an old jeans hem as the waistband, pin so that raw edge of denim shows on RS. Sew waistband in place using hem stitch or backstitch.

Fly

Cut a 1 x 4cm ($^3/_8$ x 1$^1/_2$in) strip of denim for the fly. If using old jeans, use a 4cm (1$^1/_2$in) long section from belt loops. Pin to front of trousers, directly below waistband overlap, and stitch into position.

T-shirt

Front and back (alike)

If using an old T-shirt, cut two 10cm (4in) squares using the existing hem for your hem. Otherwise, cut two rectangles 10cm (4in) wide and 14cm (5$^1/_2$in) deep. With WS facing, fold up 2cm ($^3/_4$in) at bottom edge of each square, then fold up again. Pin and stitch into position.

Short sleeves

Cut two rectangles 10cm (4in) wide and 5cm (2in) deep. Fold in half lengthways and press with steam iron.

Long sleeves

If using an old T-shirt, cut two rectangles 10cm (4in) wide and 9cm (3$^1/_2$in) deep using the existing hem for your hem. If not, cut two rectangles 10cm (4in) wide and 11cm (4$^1/_4$in) deep. Fold up 1cm ($^3/_8$in) at bottom edge of each rectangle, then fold up again. Pin and stitch into position.

Finishing

Using 5mm ($^1/_4$in) seam allowance and backstitch, pin front and back pieces RS together and then sew 2cm ($^3/_4$in) along each side of top edge to form shoulder seams and neck opening. Open out so that front and back are lying flat, then pin sleeves in place, aligning centre of sleeves with shoulder seams. Sew sleeves to body. Sew up the side and sleeve seams.

Shorts

Show off your boyfriend's legs in a pair of casual or smart shorts – or hide them by lengthening the shorts to adapt them into trousers.

Materials

Beach shorts

Two 14cm (5¹/₂in) squares of brightly coloured cotton fabric
Sharp sewing needle and matching thread
20cm (8in) cord elastic

Tailored shorts

Old pair of khaki green army trousers or 40cm (16in) square of utility-weight polycotton khaki fabric
Sharp sewing needle and matching thread
Press stud

Instructions

Beach shorts

With WS facing, fold up 1.5cm (⁵/₈in) at bottom edge of first square of fabric, then fold up again and press with steam iron. Sew along fold using hem stitch. Repeat with other square of fabric.

Measuring from top edge, mark a point 7.5cm (3in) down both side edges of each piece of fabric. With RS together and using 1cm (³/₈in) seam allowance and backstitch, sew fabric together from top edge to 7.5cm (3in) marks.

Waistband

To form channel for elastic at waist, fold down 1.5cm (⁵/₈in) from top edge, then fold down again and press with steam iron. Sew around channel, just above the folded edge, leaving a small gap for elastic to be threaded through.

With RS together, align seams at centre front and back, then sew from bottom hem to centre seam on both inside legs.

Finishing

Attach safety pin to end of elastic. Insert

pin into the gap in waistband channel and thread through. Bring ends of elastic together, place shorts on doll and pull elastic tight so that shorts fit snugly around waist. Knot the ends together and trim off excess elastic.

Tailored shorts

Using template on page 76, cut two pieces of fabric for legs of shorts. If using old pair of trousers, use existing hem and cut fabric to second fold line on template. If using fabric, hem as follows:
With WS facing, fold up 2cm (¾in) at bottom edge of first leg, then fold up again and press with steam iron. Sew along fold using hem stitch. Repeat with other leg.

Joining fabric

Measuring from top edge, mark a point 5cm (2in) down both side edges of each leg. With RS together and using 5mm (¼in) seam allowance and backstitch, sew fabric together from top edge to 5cm (2in) marks.
With RS together, align seams at centre front and back, then sew from bottom hem to centre seam on both legs.
Place shorts on doll, then fold a 1cm (³⁄₈in) pleat at front of waist on each leg; the pleats should be symmetrical and fold out towards the sides. Pin and stitch down edge of each pleat for 3cm (1¼in).

Waistband

Cut a 4cm (1½in) wide strip of fabric long enough to go around top of shorts with a 1cm (³⁄₈in) overlap at front. Fold the fabric lengthways into three sections, like an envelope. Using point of a knitting needle or similar tool, tuck in open ends of fabric strip and sew together.
Pin waistband around top of shorts, starting at centre front and allowing the other end to overlap. Sew waistband in place using hem stitch or backstitch. Sew one half of press stud to inside of overlap. Place shorts on doll, position other half of press stud on waistband to achieve a snug fit and sew in place.

Raglan Sweater

Keep your boyfriend warm and cosy in a snuggly knitted sweater.

Raglan sweater

Materials

Rowan Felted Tweed DK (50% merino wool, 25% alpaca, 25% viscose; approx 175m/191yds per 50g ball):
  1 ball in 173 Duck Egg (A)
  1 ball in 150 Rage (B)
Pair of 3.25mm (US 3) knitting needles
Tapestry needle

Tension

Approx 24 sts and 32 rows to 10cm (4in) over stocking stitch using 3.25mm (US 3) needles

Fair Isle sweater

Follow the charts on page 76 to make a Fair Isle raglan sweater, working in stocking stitch unless indicated otherwise. Change colours as shown.

Pattern

Front and back (alike)

Using B, cast on 21 sts.
Break off B and join in A.
Row 1 (RS): K1, [p1, k1] to end.
Row 2: P1, [k1, p1] to end.
Starting with a knit row, work 20 rows in stocking stitch.
Place marker at beginning and end of row.
Row 23: K2, k2togtbl, knit to last 4 sts, k2tog, k2. (19 sts)
Row 24: Purl.
Repeat last 2 rows four times more. (11 sts)
Do not cast off; slip stitches onto spare needle or stitch holder.

Sleeves (make 2)

Using B, cast on 15 sts.
Break off B and join in A.
Row 1 (RS): K1, [p1, k1] to end.
Row 2: P1, [k1, p1] to end.
Starting with a knit row, work 20 rows in stocking stitch.
Place marker at beginning and end of row.
Row 23: K2, k2togtbl, knit to last 4 sts, k2tog, k2. (13 sts)
Row 24: Purl.
Repeat last 2 rows twice more. (9 sts)
Row 29: K2, k2togtbl, k1, k2tog, k2. (7 sts)
Row 30: Purl.
Row 31: K2, slip 2, k1, p2sso, k2. (5 sts)
Row 32: Purl.
Do not cast off; slip stitches onto spare needle or stitch holder.

Neckband

With RS facing, slip pieces onto needle in following sequence: front, sleeve, back, sleeve. (32 sts)
Join in A.
Row 1 (RS): [P1, k1] twice, p2tog, [k1, p1] 4 times, k1, p2tog, k1, p1, k1, p2tog, [k1, p1] 5 times. (29 sts)
Row 2: K1, [p1, k1] to end.
Break off A and join in B.
Row 3: P1, [k1, p1] to end.
Cast off.

Finishing

Weave in loose ends. Block and press if required. Using mattress stitch, sew up the raglan seams of body and sleeves between markers. Sew up side seams and sleeves.

WHY A KNITTED
BOYFRIEND IS BETTER
THAN A REAL BOYFRIEND

1. He never says no to a cuddle
2. He never answers you back
3. He's good at washing up (he's ultra absorbent)

Knitted Jacket

Make your boyfriend look hot and cool at the same time with these funky knitted jacket designs.

Materials

Green jacket (main pattern): Rowan Tweed (100% wool; approx 118m/129yds per 50g ball):
   1 ball in 589 Hubberholme
Grey jacket (variation): Rowan Felted Tweed DK (50% merino wool, 25% alpaca, 25% viscose; approx 175m/191yds per 50g ball):
   1 ball in 172 Ancient
Pair of 3.25mm (US 3) knitting needles
Tapestry needle

Tension

Approx 24 sts and 32 rows to 10cm (4in) over stocking stitch using 3.25mm (US 3) needles

Pattern

Back and sleeves

Using the same yarn colour throughout, make a back and two sleeves as given for the raglan sweater on page 25.

Right front

Cast on 11 sts.
Row 1 (RS): K3, [p1, k1] to end.
Row 2: P1, [k1, p1] 4 times, k2.
Row 3: Knit.
Row 4: Purl to last 2 sts, k2.
Repeat last 2 rows nine times more.
Place marker at beginning and end of row.
Row 23: Knit to last 4 sts, k2tog, k2. (10 sts)
Row 24: As row 4.
Repeat last 2 rows twice more. (6 sts)
Do not cast off; slip stitches onto spare needle or stitch holder.

Left front

Cast on 11 sts.
Row 1 (RS): [K1, p1] 4 times, k3.
Row 2: K2, [p1, k1] 4 times, p1.
Row 3: Knit.
Row 4: K2, purl to end.
Repeat last 2 rows nine times more.
Place marker at beginning and end of row.
Row 23: K2, k2togtbl, knit to end.
Row 24: As row 4.
Repeat last 2 rows twice more. (6 sts)
Do not cast off; slip stitches onto spare needle or stitch holder.

Neckband

With RS facing, slip pieces onto needle in following sequence: right front, sleeve, back, sleeve, left front. (33 sts)

Row 1 (RS): K5, k2tog, k3, k2tog, k9, k2tog, k3, k2tog, k5. (29 sts)

Row 2: Knit.

Row 3: K1, m1, knit to last st, m1, k1. (31 sts)

Row 4: As row 3. (33 sts)

Cast off.

Finishing

Weave in loose ends. Block and press if required. Using mattress stitch, sew up the raglan seams of body and sleeves between markers. Sew up side seams and sleeves.

Garter stitch variation

Make a jacket with a garter stitch welt in place of 1 x 1 rib as follows:

Work as described above, but replace rows 1 and 2 of each piece with 4 rows of garter stitch (knit every row). Note that each piece will be 2 rows longer in total.

Pocket top (make 2)

Cast on 7 sts.

Work 3 rows in garter stitch.

Cast off.

Finish as above, then pin and stitch pocket tops onto front panels. Fold lapels onto RS and catch down.

Coat

Make a double-breasted flared coat for a casual night out or a single-breasted coat with straight sides for a more formal look.

Materials

Sheet of felt fabric, approx 23 x 30cm (9 x 12in)
Sharp sewing needle and matching thread

Instructions

Using templates on pages 74-75, cut out back, two fronts, two sleeves and collar from felt fabric. Make sure that you use the correct templates for the style of coat you are making.

Joining the pieces

Using 5mm (¼in) seam allowance and backstitch, pin and sew shoulders. Pin sleeves into position, aligning centre of sleeves with shoulder seams, and sew together.
Pin and sew side seams, then pin and sew sleeve seams, leaving about 1-2cm (³⁄₈-³⁄₄in) unsewn at the wrist to make it easier to slip the doll's hand through. Turn RS out and press with steam iron.

Collar and pockets

Fold collar in half and press. Align centre of collar with centre of back neck, then pin and stitch into position.
If you want to add pockets, cut out two 2.5cm (1in) squares of felt and sew onto front panels.

YOUR KNITTED BOYFRIEND'S FAVOURITE MOVIES

1. X Men: Woolverine
2. In the Loop
3. The Whole Nine Yards
4. Cast Away
5. The Dark Knit

Accessories

Add some additional bling to your boyfriend's look.
Make him look less like a sight for sore eyes ...
and give him a pair of trendy glasses or bow tie!

Materials

Long tie
3.5 x 17cm (1³/₈ x 6³/₄in) strip of fabric
Sharp sewing needle and matching thread
Press stud

Bow tie
5cm (2in) length of 4cm (1¹/₂in) wide
ribbon
Sharp sewing needle and matching thread
14cm (5¹/₂in) cord elastic

Boots and gloves
DK-weight yarn in colour of your choice
Pair of 3.25mm (US 3) knitting needles
Tapestry needle

Glasses
Reel of Scientific Wire Company
silver-plated craft wire, or colour of
your choice, 0.2mm thick

Instructions

Long tie
Following illustrations on page 75, start by
folding over 5mm (¹/₄in) lengthways on LH
side of fabric and press with steam iron.
Fold over 1cm (³/₈in) on RH side of fabric,
then fold again to create a strip approx
1cm (³/₈in) wide. Sew seam using hem
stitch. Using point of a knitting needle or
similar tool, tuck in open ends of fabric
strip and sew together.
Using illustrations as a guide, fold knot at
top to create tie effect. Sew one half of
press stud to WS of knot. Sew other half
of press stud to doll at centre front of
neckline. Press the tie onto the doll.

Bow tie
Fold ribbon into three sections, like an
envelope. Work a few stitches at one edge
to secure, then run thread through ribbon
to other edge and work a few stitches to
secure. Squeeze centre together to create
a bow tie shape and work a few stitches
to secure.

Place centre of cord elastic horizontally across WS of bow tie and stitch into position. Knot the ends of the elastic and slip over doll's head.

Boots (make 2)

Cast on 17 sts.
Knit 3 rows.
Starting with a purl row, work 5 rows in stocking stitch.
Row 9 (RS): K1, m1, k6, m1, k3, m1, k6, m1, k1. (21 sts)
Row 10: Purl.
Row 11: K9, m1, k3, m1, k9. (23 sts)
Row 12: Purl.
Shape toe as follows:
Row 13: K10, m1, k3, m1, k8, turn.
Row 14: Slip 1, p20, turn.
Row 15: Slip 1, k8, m1, k3, m1, k7, turn.
Row 16: Slip 1, p18, turn.
Row 17: Slip 1, k7, m1, k3, m1, k6, turn.
Row 18: Slip 1, p16, turn.
Row 19: Slip 1, knit to end.
Row 20: P12, p2tog, p1, p2tog, p12. (27 sts)
Cast off.
Fold cast-off edge in half and sew together. Slip boot onto doll and sew back seam.

Gloves (make 2)

Cast on 12 sts.
Starting with a knit row, work 8 rows in stocking stitch.
Row 9 (RS): K4, k2togtbl, k2tog, knit to end. (10 sts)
Row 10: Purl.
Row 11: K3, k2togtbl, k2tog, knit to end. (8 sts)
Row 12: Purl.

Break off yarn, thread through stitches on needle and pull tight, then use yarn tail to sew side seam.

Glasses

Wrap craft wire approx 10 times around two fingers. Break off, leaving a good length. Twist the loop of wire in half to make a figure-of-8, then wrap the end of wire around the centre to create bridge for nose. Cut another length of wire from reel and wrap it around frame of each lens to help hold the frames together.
Insert a large knitting needle or similar tool into each circular lens to help refine shape. Alternatively, bend the wire lenses into desired shape. Stitch into position on the doll's face.

Rock Star

This boyfriend loves his band more than anything.
He sleeps until noon and stays up all night
practising guitar solos.

Materials

Doll and jacket

Rowan Cotton Glacé (100% cotton;
approx 115m/125yds per 50g ball):
  1 ball in 730 Oyster (A)
  1 ball in 739 Dijon (B)
  1 ball in 727 Black (C)
Rowan Summer Tweed (70% silk, 30%
cotton; approx 120m/131yds per 50g ball):
  1 ball in 530 Toast (D)
Rowan Felted Tweed DK (50% merino
wool, 25% alpaca, 25% viscose; approx
175m/191yds per 50g ball):
  1 ball in 154 Ginger (E)
  1 ball in 172 Ancient (F)
Pair of 3.25mm (US 3) knitting needles
Polyester toy stuffing
Tapestry and embroidery needles
Blue and red embroidery thread for
facial features

Jeans

Old jeans or 25cm (10in) square of denim
fabric
Sharp sewing needle and white and
orange thread

Guitar

15cm (6in) square of green felt fabric
5 x 10cm (2 x 4in) piece of black felt fabric
Small pieces of grey and white felt fabric
Sharp sewing needle and thread to match
felt colours

Knitting is the new
rock and roll

Doll

Make a basic doll with a short and stocky body shape (page 8) and a 1950s quiff hairstyle (page 16), using yarn colours as follows:

Legs: Yarn B, working final row (row 30) of each leg as knit instead of purl to define bottom hem of trousers.

Feet: Yarn D.

Body and head: Use yarn C from pick-up row to end of row 26 of body, then break off C and join in A. Use yarn A to complete neck and head.

Arms and hands: Use yarn C from cast-on to end of row 26 of arms, then break off C and join in A. Use yarn A to work hands.

Soles: Yarn D.

Hair: Yarn E.

Outfit

Using F, make a knitted jacket (page 26) following the instructions for the garter stitch variation.

Make a pair of jeans (page 20) and dress the doll. (This boyfriend also has trousers knitted as part of the basic doll if you don't want to make the jeans.)

Guitar

Using templates on page 76, cut the guitar pieces from felt fabric using colours indicated. Sew front and back of guitar neck together (black felt). Pin and sew front and back of guitar body together (green felt), sandwiching end of neck between the layers. Sandwich other end of neck between the two head stock pieces (green felt). Pin and sew other sections to guitar using picture as guide.

YOUR KNITTED BOYFRIEND'S FAVOURITE ARTISTS

1. Slipknot

2. The Cardigans

3. Rage Against the Sewing Machine

4. Purl Jam

5. Knitney Spears

Surfer Dude

The only thing this totally awesome boyfriend needs is radical surf as bodacious as his brightly coloured board shorts.

Materials

Doll and shorts

Rowan Pure Wool DK (100% super wash wool; approx 130m/142yds per 50g ball):
  1 ball in 054 Tan (A)
Rowan Fine Tweed (100% wool; approx 90m/98yds per 25g ball):
  1 ball in 360 Arncliffe (B)
Rowan Big Wool (100% merino wool; approx 80m/87yds per 100g ball):
  1 ball in 048 Linen (C)
Pair of 3.25mm (US 3) knitting needles
Polyester toy stuffing
Tapestry and embroidery needles
Black and red embroidery thread for facial features
Two 14cm (5½in) squares of brightly coloured cotton fabric
20cm (8in) cord elastic
Sharp sewing needle and thread to match fabric (and felt colours below if making surfboard)

Surfboard

8 x 25cm (3¼ x 10in) piece of cardboard for template
23 x 30cm (9 x 12in) sheets of white and yellow felt fabric
1 x 8cm (⅜ x 3¼in) strip of black felt fabric
Press stud
23cm (9in) length of black DK-weight yarn

Instructions

Doll
Make a basic doll with a short and stocky body shape (page 8) and a dreadlocks hairstyle (page 18), using yarn colours as follows:
Doll: Yarn A.
Hair: Use yarn B for the hair base and yarn C for the dreadlocks.

Shorts
Dress the doll in a pair of brightly coloured beach shorts (page 22).

Surfboard
Board
Using template on page 77, cut a surfboard template from cardboard. Place cardboard template on white felt fabric and draw around it, adding 5mm (¼in) extra all around. Cut around line to make front panel, then repeat for back panel. Cut a 2cm (¾in) wide strip of yellow felt for the contrast stripe. Pin it along centre of front panel, trim to match top point of board and then sew in place using backstitch.
Sandwich the cardboard template between front and back panels and pin around outer edge. Sew layers together, leaving bottom section open for attaching ankle strap cord.

Strap and cord
Sew one half of press stud to RH side of black felt strip. Turn felt strip over so that press stud is on the LH side facing down. Sew other half of press stud to RH side. Sew length of black yarn to centre of ankle strap.
Use a tapestry needle to make a hole 2cm (¾in) up from bottom edge of surfboard, through centre of yellow strip. Use knitting needle or similar tool to widen the hole. Thread the needle with the loose end of black yarn and thread it through the hole. Tie a knot to secure. Sew along bottom edge of board.
Attach ankle strap around left ankle of doll.

Knit on, dude!

Artist

Constantly covered in bright paint, his clothes clogging up the washing machine, this boyfriend is too busy concentrating on his masterpiece to pay attention to his scruffy attire.

Materials

Doll and outfit

Rowan Cotton Glacé (100% cotton; approx 115m/125yds per 50g ball):
　1 ball in 725 Ecru (A)
　1 ball in 727 Black (B)
　1 ball in 739 Dijon (C)
Rowan Creative Focus Worsted (75% wool, 25% alpaca; approx 200m/220yds per 100g ball):
　1 ball in 500 Ebony (D)
Rowan Felted Tweed DK (50% merino wool, 25% alpaca, 25% viscose; approx 175m/191yds per 50g ball):
　1 ball in 159 Carbon (E)
Rowan Pure Wool 4ply (100% super wash wool; approx 160m/174yds per 50g ball):
　1 ball in 404 Black (F)
Pair of 3.25mm (US 3) knitting needles
Polyester toy stuffing
Tapestry and embroidery needles
Black and red embroidery thread for facial features
Crochet hook

Old T-shirt or 20cm (8in) square of jersey fabric
Sharp sewing needle and thread to match fabric
Acrylic paint in various colours
(plus brown for paintbrush below)

Easel

Three bamboo skewers, approx 25cm (10in) long
Two lolly sticks, approx 11cm (4¼in) long
Craft knife, superglue and Blu-Tack

Canvas

9 x 11.5cm (3½ x 4½in) rectangle of cardboard
11 x 13.5cm (4¼ x 5¼in) rectangle of white felt fabric

Paintbrush

Short bamboo skewer
Short length of beige yarn
50cm (20in) silver-plated craft wire, 0.2mm thick
Craft knife and superglue

Palette

8cm (3¹/₄in) square of cardboard for template
8 x 16cm (3¹/₄ x 6¹/₄in) rectangle of grey felt fabric
Small scraps of red, yellow, turquoise and lime felt fabric
Thread to match felt fabrics

Instructions

Doll

Make a basic doll with a short and slim body shape (page 8), a ponytail hairstyle (page 18) and a goatee (page 19), using yarn colours as follows:

Legs: Yarn B, working final row (row 30) of each leg as knit instead of purl to define bottom hem of trousers.

Feet: Yarn C.

Body and head: Yarn A.

Arms and hands: Yarn A.

Soles: Yarn C.

Hair and goatee: Yarn D, with about four strands of yarn E in the ponytail for a grey streak.

Outfit

Make a short- or long-sleeved T-shirt (page 21) and add the finishing touch by spattering it with brightly coloured acrylic paint. Dress the doll.

Easel

Glue pointed tips of two skewers together. Insert flat ends of skewers into Blu-Tack so that they stand upright and allow to dry. Make pencil marks 7cm (2³/₄in) up from base of skewers. Glue a lolly stick across the skewers at the pencil marks, making sure that it is evenly positioned. Allow to dry.

Use a craft knife to trim the second lolly stick to approx 6cm (2¹/₂in) long by cutting off each curved end. Mark the skewers 4.5cm (1³/₄in) down from top. Glue trimmed lolly stick across marked points and allow to dry.

Glue tip of third skewer to back of first two skewers to make a tripod and allow to dry.

Canvas

Place cardboard in centre of felt fabric and draw around it. Remove cardboard and cut a 1cm (³/₈in) square from each corner of the felt so that you are left with flaps along each of the four sides. Fold the flaps over and press with a steam iron. Place cardboard on WS of felt fabric, fold over the flaps and stitch each of the corners together.

Paintbrush

Cut a 4cm (1½in) section of bamboo skewer, paint it brown and allow to dry. Wrap the beige yarn around your finger approx 10 times. Remove from finger and wind remaining tail of yarn around base. Fold silver wire in half and wrap it a few times around base of yarn.

Insert painted skewer into wrapped base of yarn and continue wrapping wire around yarn and skewer. Once all the wire has been wrapped around, add a spot of glue to secure and allow to dry.

Once dry, trim the yarn to look like the bristles of a paintbrush.

Palette

Using template on page 79, cut a palette template from cardboard. Place cardboard template onto grey felt fabric and draw around it, adding 5mm (¼in) extra all around. Cut around line to make front panel, then repeat for back panel.

Cut a few small random shapes of coloured felt. Place them on front panel and stitch into position. Sandwich cardboard template between front and back panels, then pin around outer edge. Sew layers together using backstitch.

YOUR KNITTED
BOYFRIEND LOVES
YOU BECAUSE

1. You're a knitphomaniac!

2. He's scared of your pointy sticks!

3. You always have him in stitches!

4. You've got a tight-knit group of friends!

5. You offer many purls of wisdom!

Fireman

He may be a sweltering hot hero every day for someone else, but when this fireman boyfriend comes home at the end of the day it'll be you that needs a cold shower...

Materials

Rowan Cotton Glacé (100% cotton; approx 115m/125yds per 50g ball):
- 1 ball in 843 Toffee (A)
- 1 ball in 727 Black (B)
- 1 ball in 831 Dawn Grey (D)

Rowan Kid Classic (70% lambswool, 22% kid mohair, 8% polyamide; approx 140m/153yds per 50g ball):
- 1 ball in 846 Nightly (C)

Rowan Creative Focus Worsted (75% wool, 25% alpaca; approx 200m/220yds per 100g ball):
- 1 ball in 3810 Saffron (E)

Pair of 3.25mm (US 3) and 3mm (US 2) knitting needles
Polyester toy stuffing
Tapestry and embroidery needles
Black and red embroidery thread for facial features, plus brown for stubble
Old pair of beige jeans or 50cm (20in) square of similar fabric
23 x 30cm (9 x 12in) sheets of yellow and grey felt fabric

Sharp sewing needle and thread to match fabric and felt colours
20cm (8in) cord elastic

Instructions

Doll

Using 3.25mm (US 3) needles, make a basic doll with a tall and stocky body shape (page 8), a bald head and stubble (pages 16 and 19), using yarn colours as follows:

Legs and feet: Yarn A.

Body and head: Use yarn D from pick-up row to end of row 32 of body, then break off D and join in A. Use yarn A to complete neck and head.

Arms and hands: Use yarn D from cast-on to end of row 6 of arms, then break off D and join in A. Use yarn A to complete arms and hands.

Soles: Yarn A.

Stubble: Brown embroidery thread.

Trousers

Using template on page 78, cut front and back of trousers from fabric. If using old pair of jeans, use existing hem and cut to fold line on template.

With RS together and using 5mm (¹/₄in) seam allowance and backstitch, pin and sew side seams and then inside leg seams. If using fabric rather than jeans, fold up 1.5cm (⁵/₈in) at bottom edge of each leg and stitch.

To form channel for elastic at waist, fold down 1.5cm (⁵/₈in) from top edge and press with steam iron. Sew around channel, just above the selvedge, leaving a small gap for elastic to be threaded through.

Visibility strips

Cut two 1.5cm (⁵/₈in) wide strips of yellow felt fabric and two 5mm (¹/₄in) strips of grey felt, each long enough to fit around trouser leg. Pin and stitch a grey strip along centre of each yellow strip. Pin and stitch around trouser legs 2.5cm (1in) up from bottom.

Waistband

Attach safety pin to end of elastic. Insert pin into the gap in waistband channel and thread through. Bring ends of elastic together, place trousers on doll and pull elastic tight so that trousers fit snugly around waist. Knot the ends together and trim off excess elastic.

Jacket

Using templates on pages 78-79, cut out back, two fronts and two sleeves from fabric. With RS together and using 5mm (¹/₄in) seam allowance and backstitch, pin and sew shoulder seams. Pin sleeves into position, aligning centre of sleeves with shoulder seams, and sew in place. Pin and sew side seams, then sleeve seams.

With WS facing, fold up 1cm (³/₈in) hem at bottom of jacket and sleeves and stitch to secure. Fold back 1cm (³/₈in) at each front edge, then fold again. Press with steam iron and sew using hem stitch. Turn RS out and press again.

Collar

Cut a 4cm (1¹/₂in) wide strip of fabric long enough to go around neckline plus 1cm (³/₈in) extra for tucking in ends. Fold the fabric lengthways into three sections, like an envelope. Matching centre of collar with centre of back neck, pin and stitch into position using hem stitch or backstitch. Using point of a knitting needle or similar tool, tuck in open ends of fabric strip to align with front edges of jacket and sew together.

Visibility strips

Sew yellow and grey felt visibility strips around sleeves and bottom of jacket, just above the hems, in the same way as for the trousers.

Boots

Using B, make a pair of boots (page 31).

Helmet

Using 3.25mm (US 3) needles and E, cast on 34 sts.

Work 10 rows in stocking stitch.

Row 11 (RS): K1, [k2togtbl, k4, k2tog] to last st, k1. (26 sts)

Row 12: Purl.

Row 13: K1, [k2togtbl, k2, k2tog] to last st, k1. (18 sts)

Row 14: Purl.

Row 15: K1, [k2togtbl, k2tog] to last st, k1. (10 sts)

Row 16: Purl.

Break off yarn and thread through sts on needle.

Make brim as follows:

With RS facing and using E, pick up and knit 34 sts along cast-on edge.

Row 1 (WS): Knit.

Row 2: K2, [knit into front and back of next st, k1] to last 2 sts, knit to end. (49 sts)

Row 3: Knit.

Cast off.

Sew up back seam and weave in loose ends.

Hose

Using 3mm (US 2) needles and C, cast on 120 sts.

Cast off.

Nozzle

Using 3.25mm (US 3) needles and B, cast on 6 sts.

Knit 2 rows, then work 6 rows in stocking stitch.

Row 9: K2, m1, k2, m1, k2. (8 sts)

Knit 2 rows.

Cast off.

Weave in loose ends. Wrap nozzle around one end of hose, with wider cast-off edge of nozzle to the outside. Sew side edges of nozzle together and work a few stitches through nozzle and hose to secure.

Everyone loves a knitted man in uniform

Computer Geek

Throw away his nerdy old anorak and give this boffin-of-a-boyfriend some classy, geek-chic style. He'll be too busy staring at his computer screen to notice, but do it anyway!

Materials

Doll and sweater
Rowan Cotton Glacé (100% cotton; approx 115m/125yds per 50g ball):
- 1 ball in 725 Ecru (A)
- 1 ball in 831 Dawn Grey (B)
- 1 ball in 727 Black (C)

Rowan Pure Wool DK (100% super wash wool; approx 130m/142yds per 50g ball):
- 1 ball in 018 Earth (D)

Rowan Felted Tweed DK (50% merino wool, 25% alpaca, 25% viscose; approx 175m/191yds per 50g ball):
- 1 ball in 161 Avocado (E)

Pair of 3.25mm (US 3) knitting needles
Polyester toy stuffing
Tapestry and embroidery needles
Blue and red embroidery thread for facial features

Collar, bow tie and glasses
15cm (6in) square of checked fabric
5cm (2in) length of 4cm (1½in) wide ribbon
14cm (5½in) cord elastic
Sharp sewing needle and thread to match fabric and ribbon
Reel of Scientific Wire Company silver-plated craft wire, 0.2mm thick

Calculator
Scrap of cardboard for template
12cm (4¾in) square of black felt fabric
6cm (2½in) square of light grey felt fabric
Scraps of green and red felt fabric for buttons
Sharp sewing needle and thread to match felt colours

KNIT 2 TOG
4EVA

Instructions

Doll

Make a basic doll with a short and slim body shape (page 8) and a short back and sides hairstyle (page 14), using yarn colours as follows:

Legs: Yarn B, working final row (row 30) of each leg as knit instead of purl to define bottom hem of trousers.
Feet: Yarn C.
Body and head: Yarn A.
Arms and hands: Yarn A.
Soles: Yarn C.
Hair: Yarn D.

Outfit

Using E throughout, make a raglan sweater (page 24).

To add a collar, cut an 8 x 12cm (3¹/₄ x 4³/₄in) rectangle from checked fabric. With RS together, fold in half lengthways. Using 1cm (³/₈in) seam allowance and backstitch, sew short side edges together. Turn RS out, using a knitting needle to push out the points. Press with a steam iron.

Fold collar in half lengthways and press again. Pin raw edge of collar to inside of sweater's neckline, making sure that the points of the collar are evenly spaced at the front. Sew the collar to the sweater. Dress the doll and give him a tartan bow tie (page 30) and pair of glasses (page 31).

Calculator

Cutting the pieces

Using template on page 76, cut a calculator template from cardboard. Bend top curved section along fold line, then open out flat again. Place cardboard template on black felt fabric and draw around it, adding 5mm (¹/₄in) extra all around. Cut around line to make front panel, then repeat for back panel.

Cut a 1 x 3cm (³/₈ x 1¹/₄in) rectangle of grey felt for the screen and a 2 x 3cm (³/₄ x 1¹/₄in) rectangle of grey felt for the buttons. Cut two 5mm (¹/₄in) squares of green felt and two of red felt.

Assembling

Sew screen across top rounded section of front panel, then sew green and red squares to left-hand side and grey button section to right-hand side below the fold line.

Thread tapestry needle with black yarn and work three horizontal and two vertical lines across lower grey panel to create buttons. Using black thread and sewing needle, stitch down the black yarn grid on the button panel. Sandwich cardboard template between front and back panels and pin around outer edge. Sew layers together using backstitch, then bend top screen section at a slight angle.

Superhero

He might be amazing at saving the world, but this superhero boyfriend is also the only man who can pull off the impossible – make knitted underpants-over-tights look good!

Materials

Rowan Pure Wool DK (100% super wash wool; approx 130m/142yds per 50g ball):
- 1 ball in 054 Tan (A)
- 1 ball in 018 Earth (B)

Rowan Cotton Glacé (100% cotton; approx 115m/125yds per 50g ball):
- 1 ball in 741 Poppy (C)
- 1 ball in 727 Black (D)
- 1 ball in 849 Winsor (E)

Pair of 3.25mm (US 3) knitting needles
Polyester toy stuffing
Tapestry and embroidery needles
Black and red embroidery thread for facial features
Crochet hook
20cm (8in) craft wire
3 x 8cm (1¼ x 3¼in) piece of turquoise felt fabric
Sharp sewing needle and turquoise thread

Instructions

Doll

Make a basic doll with a tall and stocky body shape (page 8) and a slicked-back hairstyle (page 18), using yarn colours as follows:

Legs and feet: Yarn C.

Body and head: Use yarn C from pick-up row to end of row 32 of body, then break off C and join in A. Use yarn A to complete neck and head.

Arms and hands: Use yarn C from cast-on to end of row 30 of arms, then break off C and join in A. Use yarn A to work hands.

Soles: Yarn D.

Hair: Yarn B.

Saving the world, one dropped stitch at a time

Pants

Using E, cast on 19 sts.

Starting with a knit row, work 6 rows in stocking stitch.

Row 7 (RS): K1, k2togtbl, knit to last 3 sts, k2tog, k1. (17 sts)

Row 8: P1, p2tog, purl to last 3 sts, p2togtbl, p1. (15 sts)

Repeat last 2 rows twice more. (7 sts)

Row 13: As row 7. (5 sts)

Row 14: P1, p3tog, p1. (3 sts)

Work 2 rows in stocking stitch.

Row 17: K1, m1, k1, m1, k1. (5 sts)

Row 18: P1, m1, purl to last st, m1, p1. (7 sts)

Row 19: K1, m1, knit to last st, m1, k1. (9 sts)

Repeat last 2 rows twice more. (17 sts)

Row 24: As row 18. (19 sts)

Work 6 rows in stocking stitch.

Cast off.

Fold up pants with cast-on and cast-off edges together. Sew first 3 rows on each side together to form side seams. Dress the doll in the pants.

Cape

Using E, cast on 13 sts.

Row 1 (RS): Knit.

Row 2: K2, purl to last 2 sts, k2.

Row 3: [K3, m1] twice, k1, [m1, k3] twice. (17 sts)

Row 4: As row 2.

Row 5: Knit.

Row 6: As row 2.

Row 7: K3, m1, k5, m1, k1, m1, k5, m1, k3. (21 sts)

Row 8: As row 2.

Row 9: Knit.

Repeat last 2 rows once more, then row 2 once again.

Row 13: K3, m1, k7, m1, k1, m1, k7, m1, k3. (25 sts)

Knit 2 rows.

Cast off.

Cut two lengths of craft wire 2cm (³/₄in) longer than side edges of cape. Insert on WS, weaving in and out of garter stitch side edges. Fold over ends of wire and stitch into position to secure. Stitch cape along back neck of doll and bend into desired position.

Mask

Using template on page 76, cut the mask out of felt fabric. Place across doll's face, making sure that eyeholes match up with eyes. Pin and stitch into position at the side edges.

Sports Star

No matter what games he's playing, this sports star boyfriend is constantly on the run. You might as well make him look the part as he does so. On your marks, get set, go!

Materials

Doll and outfit

Rowan Cotton Glacé (100% cotton; approx 115m/125yds per 50g ball):
- 1 ball in 730 Oyster (A)
- 1 ball in 726 Bleached (B)

Rowan Felted Tweed DK (50% merino wool, 25% alpaca, 25% viscose; approx 175m/191yds per 50g ball):
- 1 ball in 154 Ginger (C)

Pair of 3.25mm (US 3) knitting needles
Polyester toy stuffing
Tapestry and embroidery needles
Green and red embroidery thread for facial features
Small white shirt button, approx 1cm (³⁄₈in) diameter

Accessories

Rowan Cotton Glacé (100% cotton; approx 115m/125yds per 50g ball):
- 1 ball in 727 Black (D)
- 1 ball in 725 Ecru (E)
- 1 ball in 831 Dawn Grey (F)

Rowan Handknit Cotton (100% cotton; approx 85m/93yds per 50g ball):
- 1 ball in 219 Gooseberry (G)

Two 2.25mm (US 1) double-pointed needles for working i-cord
30cm (12in) craft wire, 1mm thick
Pliers
Reel of Scientific Wire Company silver-plated craft wire, 0.2mm thick
4cm (1¹⁄₂in) square of black felt fabric
Sharp sewing needle and black thread

Game, stitch and match

Instructions

Doll

Make a basic doll with a tall and slim body shape (page 8) and a curly hairstyle (page 17), using yarn colours as follows:

Legs and feet: Use yarn B from cast-on to end of row 8 as directed. Continue using B to work first 8 rows of stocking stitch for left leg, but work eighth row in knit instead of purl to define bottom hem of shorts. Break off B and join in A. Starting with a knit row, work 28 rows in stocking stitch to complete left leg. Break off A and join in B to work left foot. Work right leg and foot in matching colours.

Body and head: Use yarn B from pick-up row to end of row 32 of body, then break off B and join in A. Use yarn A to complete neck and head.

Arms and hands: Use yarn B from cast-on to end of row 6 of arms, then break off B and join in A. Use yarn A to complete arms and hands.

Soles: Yarn B.

Hair: Yarn C.

Outfit

Collar

Using B, cast on 5 sts.

Knit 2 rows.

Row 3: K1, k2togtbl, k2. (4 sts)

Row 4: Knit.

Row 5: K1, k2togtbl, k1. (3 sts)

Knit 25 rows.

Row 31: K1, m1, k2. (4 sts)

Row 32: Knit.

Row 33: K1, m1, k3. (5 sts)

Row 34: Knit.

Cast off.

Placket

Using B, cast on 3 sts.

Knit 9 rows.

Cast off.

Waistband

Using B, cast on 3 sts.

Knit 51 rows.

Cast off.

Finishing

Pin and stitch collar around neckline of doll. Sew shirt button onto placket, then sew placket to centre front neckline with button at top. Wrap waistband around body and sew ends together, then sew to body.

Tennis racket

Frame

Using double-pointed needles and B, cast on 3 sts and work i-cord as follows:

Row 1: Knit.

Do not turn; slide the stitches to other end of needle.

Pull yarn tightly across back of work and knit one more row.

Repeat until 80 rows have been worked or length is 27cm (10¾in). Cast off.

Handle grip

Using D, cast on 8 sts.

Work 8 rows in stocking stitch.

Cast off.

Finishing

Thread the 1mm-thick craft wire through i-cord frame. Using pliers, fold up excess wire and squeeze together, making as flat as possible. Bend into tennis racket shape, with straight handle section approx 3cm (1¹/₄in) long.

Wrap the knitted handle grip around straight handle section of frame and stitch into position.

To add strings, thread tapestry needle with yarn E. Insert needle up through i-cord on one side of frame, just above handle. Take the needle horizontally across to opposite side and insert into i-cord there. Move the needle a little farther along through the i-cord frame and then bring it back out. Repeat this process to add approx 12 horizontal strings up to top of frame. Repeat to add vertical strings, weaving the yarn over and under the horizontal strings. Fasten off.

Tennis ball

Using G, cast on 3 sts.

Work as follows: K1, [k1, p1] 3 times into next st, [turn and p6, turn and k6] twice, turn and p6, turn and slip 3, k3tog, p3sso st resulting from k3tog, k1, turn, p3tog. Break off yarn, leaving a good length tail, and thread through stitch on needle. Thread tapestry needle with tail from cast-off and sew bobble to form tennis ball. Repeat with cast-on tail.

Trophy

Use yarn F and silver-plated craft wire together throughout trophy pattern.

Cup

Cast on 26 sts.

Starting with a knit row, work 8 rows in stocking stitch.

Row 9 (RS): K3, k2togtbl, [k2, k2togtbl] to last st, k1. (20 sts)

Row 10: Purl.

Row 11: K2, k2togtbl, [k1, k2togtbl] to last st, k1. (14 sts)

Row 12: Purl.

Row 13: K1, [k2togtbl] to last st, k1. (8 sts)

Starting and ending with a purl row, work 7 rows in stocking stitch.

Row 21: K2, [m1, k1] to end. (14 sts)

Cast off.

Handle (make 2)

Cast on 10 sts, then cast off.

Finishing

Using mattress stitch and yarn F only, sew side seam of trophy. Mould into shape, then sew handles onto sides. Cut a 3cm (1¹/₄in) circle of black felt fabric and sew to base of trophy using black thread.

Intrepid Explorer

Adventurous boyfriends usually turn up at your door covered in mud, dust and cobwebs! But if your boyfriend has a habit of dashing off to some exotic, faraway island you might as well make him look dashing too! Especially if he takes you with him!

Materials

Doll and outfit
Rowan Pure Wool DK (100% super wash wool; approx 130m/142yds per 50g ball):
- 1 ball in 054 Tan (A)
- 1 ball in 018 Earth (B)

Rowan Cotton Glacé (100% cotton; approx 115m/125yds per 50g ball):
- 1 ball in 739 Dijon (C)
- 1 ball in 727 Black (D)

Rowan Tweed (100% wool; approx 118m/129yds per 50g ball):
- 1 ball in 589 Hubberholme (E)

Anchor Tapestry wool (100% wool; approx 10m per skein):
- 1 skein in 9314 (F)

Pair of 3.25mm (US 3) knitting needles
Polyester toy stuffing
Tapestry and embroidery needles
Black and red embroidery thread for facial features

Old pair of khaki green army trousers or 40cm (16in) square of utility-weight polycotton khaki fabric
Press stud
10cm (4in) square of black felt fabric for hat
Sharp sewing needle and thread to match fabric and felt colours (including for items below)

Map
10cm (4in) squares of felt fabric in pale blue (A), mid-blue (B), beige (C), green and oatmeal (E)
Blue and ochre embroidery thread

Compass
5cm (2in) square of black felt fabric
2cm (¾in) square of grey felt fabric
Small amount of red and white embroidery thread

Instructions

Doll

Make a basic doll with a tall and stocky body shape (page 8), a shoulder-length hairstyle (page 18) and a moustache and sideburns (page 19), using yarn colours as follows:

Legs: Yarn A.

Feet: Yarn D.

Body and head: Use yarn C from cast-on to end of row 32 of body, then break off C and join in A. Use yarn A to complete neck and head.

Arms and hands: Use yarn C from cast-on to end of row 6 or arms, then break off C and join in A. Use yarn A to complete arms and hands.

Soles: Yarn D.

Hair: Yarn B.

Outfit

Socks (make 2)

Using F, cast on 17 sts.

Row 1: K1, [p1, k1] to end.

Row 2: P1, [k1, p1] to end.

Row 3: As row 1.

Cast off.

Sew short edges together and slip onto doll's ankles.

Jacket and shorts

Using E, make a knitted jacket following the main pattern instructions (page 26). Make a pair of tailored shorts using khaki fabric (page 23). Dress the doll.

Hat

Crown

Using D, cast on 8 sts.

Row 1 (WS): Purl.

Row 2 (RS): Knit into front and back of each st. (16 sts)

Row 3: Purl.

Row 4: As row 2. (32 sts)

Starting and ending with a purl row, work 9 rows in stocking stitch.

Cast off.

Sew up side seam, leaving cast-on edge open.

Turn hat WS out, flatten with side seam to the left so that cast-on edge stitches are together at the top and then sew along the top using backstitch. This will help give the hat its shape.

Weave in all loose ends.

Brim

Using template on page 79, cut a circular ring from black felt fabric. Snip small cuts around inside of ring as marked on template. Fold snips upwards and place around cast-off edge of knitted section. Pin and sew into position using backstitch. Fold up sides of brim, making sure that knitted seam is to the front. Pin and catch each side in place with a few stitches. Press top of front seam with fingers to help create shape of hat.

Using D, cast on 24 sts.
Knit 2 rows.
Row 3 (RS): K1, k2togtbl, k7, k2togtbl,
k2tog, k7, k2tog, k1. (20 sts)
Starting and ending with a purl row, work
8 rows in stocking stitch.
Row 7: K1, k2togtbl, k5, k2togtbl, k2tog,
k5, k2tog, k1. (16 sts)
Starting with a purl row, work 2 rows in
stocking stitch.
Cast off.

Finishing
With WS facing, lay flat and roll RH edge
to centre to form first lens. Sew into place,
then repeat with LH edge. Weave in all
loose ends. To make cord for hanging
binoculars around doll's neck, cut a 25cm
(10in) length of yarn and attach ends
inside cast-off edges.
Help to refine the shape if necessary by
inserting a large knitting needle into each
lens piece from cast-on edge.

Using templates on page 79, cut map
sections from felt fabric in colours
indicated. Place section B onto section A,
aligning the edge of B with the dotted line
marked on A. Pin and stitch into position
using backstitch. Repeat this process to
add sections C and D.
Mark six horizontal lines approx 7mm
($^5/_{16}$in) apart on map. Stitch along these
lines using blue thread and backstitch.
Repeat to add vertical lines. Embroider
contour lines on the green section using
ochre thread. Sew in all loose ends.
Trim remaining square of felt fabric to
match map, then sew together around the
edge using backstitch.

Compass
Cut two 2 x 2.5cm ($^3/_4$ x 1in) rectangles of
black felt fabric. Using short edge as top
of compass, embroider a white capital N
at centre top edge of first black rectangle.
Cut a 1cm ($^3/_8$in) circle from grey felt fabric
and stitch to black rectangle below the N.
Embroider a two-colour compass needle
vertically across the grey circle, with a
red satin stitch pointing north and a white
satin stitch pointing south.
Place second rectangle of black felt
underneath and sew together around
outer edge using backstitch.

Behind every great
knitter is a great
knitted boyfriend

Spaceman

This boyfriend is forever looking at the stars contemplating life, the universe and everything. Or he just likes playing with rockets. Either way, he'll need the perfect outfit when zooming through space.

Materials

Rowan Cotton Glacé (100% cotton; approx 115m/125yds per 50g ball):
    1 ball in 843 Toffee (A)
    1 ball in 831 Dawn Grey (B)
    1 ball in 726 Bleached (C)
Rowan Creative Focus Worsted (75% wool, 25% alpaca; approx 200m/220yds per 100g ball):
    1 ball in 500 Ebony (D)
Pair of 3.25mm (US 3) knitting needles
Two 3.25mm (US 3) double-pointed needles for working i-cord
Polyester toy stuffing
Tapestry and embroidery needles
Black and red embroidery thread for facial features
50cm (20in) square of white cotton fabric
20cm (8in) squares of white and grey felt fabric
10cm (4in) square of red felt fabric
Scraps of black and blue felt fabric
Sharp sewing needle and thread to match fabric and felt colours
5 press studs

Reel of Scientific Wire Company silver-plated craft wire, 0.2mm thick
20cm (8in) cord elastic
Clear plastic round yoghurt pot

Instructions

Doll
Make a basic doll with a short and slim body shape (page 8) and an afro hairstyle (page 15), using yarn colours as follows:
Doll: Yarn A.
Hair: Yarn D.

Gloves and boots
Using B, make a pair of gloves and boots (page 31).

Space suit
Using templates on page 77, cut space suit front, back and two sleeves from white fabric.
With RS together and using 5mm ($^1/_4$in) seam allowance and backstitch, pin and sew shoulder seams. Pin sleeves into

position, aligning centre of sleeves with shoulder seams, and sew in place.

Pin and sew side seams, then sleeve seams and inside leg seams. Fold up 1cm (³/₈in) hem at bottom of each leg and sleeve and sew in place. Turn RS out. Cut collar and left and right plackets from white felt fabric. Pin and stitch placket to back opening, with narrow strip on left and wider strip on right, making sure that they match up. Pin and stitch collar around neckline. Sew press stud to back opening of collar.

Sew one half of another press stud to front of each sleeve, 5mm (¹/₄in) up from bottom hem and 1.5cm (⁵/₈in) up from sleeve seam. Sew other half of press stud 5mm (¹/₄in) further along from sleeve seam. Cut a 7mm x 8cm (⁵/₁₆ x 3¹/₄in) strip of red felt fabric and sew around middle of each sleeve.

Front panel

Cut a 3.5 x 4.5cm (1³/₈ x 1³/₄in) rectangle from white felt fabric. Cut two 1cm (³/₈in) circles from black felt, plus one red and one blue felt circle slightly smaller than the black. Sew coloured circles onto black ones, then stitch onto front panel using picture as a guide. Cut three small rectangles from grey felt and sew onto front panel.

Tube (make 2)

Using double-pointed needles and B, cast on 3 sts and work i-cord as follows:
Row 1: Knit.
Do not turn; slide the stitches to other end of needle.

Pull yarn tightly across back of work and knit one more row.

Repeat until 30 rows have been worked in total.

Cast off and weave in loose ends.

Sew end of one tube to red felt circle on front panel, and end of second tube to blue circle. Pin and stitch panel to front of space suit.

Helmet

Using C, cast on 32 sts. Knit 2 rows.
Row 3 (RS): Knit.
Row 4: K2, purl to last 2 sts, k2.
Repeat last 2 rows five times more.
Row 15: K7, [k2tog, k5] 3 times, k2tog, k2. (28 sts)
Row 16 and all WS rows: As row 2.
Row 17: K6, [k2tog, k4] 3 times, k2tog, k2. (24 sts)
Row 19: K5, [k2tog, k3] 3 times, k2tog, k2. (20 sts)
Row 21: K4, [k2tog, k2] 3 times, k2tog, k2. (16 sts)
Row 23: K3, [k2tog, k1] 3 times, k2tog, k2. (12 sts)
Row 25: K2, [k2tog] to last 2 sts, k2. (8 sts)
Break off yarn and thread through stitches on needle. Pull tight and secure the end.

Visor

Using template on page 77, cut visor from yoghurt pot. Using sharp needle, punch holes around outer edge of visor, 5mm (¹/₄in) in from edge. Sew knitted section to visor.

Cut a 2cm (³/₄in) wide neckband from grey felt fabric, long enough to go around bottom edge of helmet with small overlap at back. Sew into position.

Sew one half of a press stud to space suit collar in line with each shoulder seam, then sew other half of press studs to inside of helmet neckband to match.

Rocket (make 2)

Use yarn B and craft wire together throughout, cast on 18 sts.

Starting with a knit row, work 21 rows in stocking stitch.

Row 22 (WS): Knit.

Row 23 (RS): K3, [k2togtbl, k2] 3 times, k2togtbl, k1. (14 sts)

Row 24: Purl.

Row 25: K2, [k2togtbl, k1] 3 times, k2togtbl, k1. (10 sts)

Row 26: Purl.

Row 27: K1, [k2togtbl] to last st, k1. (6 sts)

Row 28: Purl.

Break off yarn and wire and thread through sts on needle, leaving long enough tail of yarn B to sew side seam. Tuck tail end of wire into the inside. Insert stuffing and mould into shape. Cut two 3cm (1¼in) circles of grey felt and sew to base of each rocket.

Making backpack

Sew rockets together between base and row of garter stitch (row 22).

Cut cord elastic in half to make arm straps. Position the straps on back of rocket pack towards outer edges. For each strap, thread tapestry needle with elastic, insert needle into rocket two rows below shaping and then bring it out 3cm (1¼in) further down. Knot ends of elastic together and tuck knot inside knitting. Sew the tubes attached to front panel to back of each rocket, just above base.

Doctor

Scrub up this boyfriend and turn him from 'Doctor Who?' to 'Doctor McDreamy' with a style that gets pulses racing in a healthy way.

Materials

Doll and collar
Rowan Cotton Glacé (100% cotton; approx 115m/125yds per 50g ball):
- 1 ball in 730 Oyster (A)
- 1 ball in 727 Black (B)
- 1 ball in 749 Sky (C)
- 1 ball in 843 Toffee (D)

Rowan Felted Tweed DK (50% merino wool, 25% alpaca, 25% viscose; approx 175m/191yds per 50g ball):
- 1 ball in 181 Mineral (E)

Pair of 3.25mm (US 3) knitting needles
Polyester toy stuffing
Tapestry and embroidery needles
Blue and red embroidery thread for facial features
Sharp sewing needle and thread to match fabric and felt colours if making items below

Lab coat
23 x 30cm (9 x 12in) sheet of white felt fabric

Tie
3.5 x 17cm (1³/₈ x 6³/₄in) strip of patterned fabric
Press stud

Stethoscope
Small pieces of black and grey felt fabric
14cm (5¹/₂in) silver craft wire
Pliers

He'll have you
in stitches

Instructions

Doll

Make a basic doll with a tall and slim body shape (page 8) and a side parting hairstyle (page 15), using yarn colours as follows:

Legs: Yarn B, working final row (row 36) of each leg as knit instead of purl to define bottom hem of trousers.

Feet: Yarn D.

Body and head: Use yarn C from pick-up row to end of row 32 of body, then break off C and join in A. Use yarn A to complete neck and head.

Arms and hands: Use yarn C from cast-on to end of row 30 of arms, then break off C and join in A. Use yarn A to work hands.

Soles: Yarn D.

Hair: Yarn E.

Outfit

Using C, make a collar as given for the Sports Star boyfriend on page 52. Pin and stitch collar around neckline of doll, then sew one half of press stud to centre front neckline.

Make a long tie (page 30) and sew other half of press stud to WS of knot. Press tie onto doll.

Using white felt, make a lab coat with straight sides and pockets (page 28), then dress the doll.

Stethoscope

Using B, cast on 22 sts.

Cast off 6 sts, slip st used to cast off back onto LH needle, cast on 6 sts, then cast off to end.

Weave in loose ends.

Insert craft wire through top V section of the knitted cord. Making sure that the wire is even, bend the middle to form a V-shape. Use pliers to bend 1cm (³⁄₈in) at ends of wire inwards at 90-degree angle.

Cut two 1 x 2cm (³⁄₈ x ³⁄₄in) strips of black felt fabric. Wrap them around bent ends of the wire and stitch to secure.

Cut two 1cm (³⁄₈in) circles from grey felt fabric. Sandwich the loose end of the knitted cord between the circles and sew together.

YOUR KNITTED
BOYFRIEND'S FAVOURITE
TV SHOWS

1. Made Men
2. The Knitted Dead
3. The Stitch of It
4. The Big Bind Theory
5. Knit Rider

Techniques

Working from a pattern

Before starting any pattern, always read it through. This will give you an idea of how the design is structured and the techniques that are involved. Each pattern includes the following basic elements:

Materials
This section gives a list of materials required, including the amount of yarn, the sizes of needles and any extras. The yarn amounts specified are based on average requirements and are therefore approximate.

Abbreviations
Knitting instructions are normally given in an abbreviated form, which saves valuable space.

In this book the most commonly used abbreviations are listed on page 80.

Project instructions
Before starting to knit, read the instructions carefully to understand the abbreviations used, how the design is structured and in which order each piece is worked. However, there may be some parts of the pattern that only become clear when you are knitting them.

Asterisks or square brackets are used to indicate the repetition of a sequence of stitches. For example: *k3, p1; rep from * to end. This means, knit three stitches, then purl one stitch, then repeat this sequence to the end of the row. It could also be written: [k3, p1] to end.

When you put your knitting aside, always mark where you are on the pattern; it is better to be safe than sorry, especially if a complex stitch is involved.

Tension and selecting correct needle size
Tension can differ quite dramatically between knitters. This is because of the way that the needles and the yarn are held.

If your tension does not match that stated in the pattern, you should change your needle size following this simple rule:

- If your knitting is too loose, your tension will read that you have fewer stitches and rows than the given tension, and you will need to change to a thinner needle, or a smaller needle size, to make the stitch size smaller.
- If your knitting is too tight, your tension will read that you have more stitches and rows than the given tension, and you will need to change to a thicker needle, or a larger needle size, to make the stitch size bigger.

Finishing
The finishing section in each project will tell you how to join the knitted pieces together. Always follow the recommended sequence.

Making a slip knot

A slip knot is the basis of all casting-on techniques and is therefore the starting point for almost everything you do in knitting.

1 Wind the yarn around two fingers twice, as shown. Insert a knitting needle through the first (front) strand and under the second (back) one.

2 Using the needle, pull the back strand through the front one to form a loop. Holding the loose ends of the yarn with your left hand, pull the needle upwards, thus tightening the knot.

Casting on

Casting on is the term used for making a row of stitches to be used as a foundation for your knitting.

1 Place the slip knot on the needle, leaving a long tail, and hold the needle in your right hand.

2 *Wind the loose end of the yarn around your thumb from front to back. Place the ball end of the yarn over your left forefinger.

3 Insert the point of the needle under the loop on your thumb. With your right index finger, take the ball end of the yarn over the point of the needle.

4 Pull a loop through to form the first stitch. Remove your left thumb from the yarn. Pull the loose end to secure the stitch. Repeat from * until the required number of stitches has been cast on.

The Basic Stitches

The knit and purl stitches form the basis of all knitted fabrics.

Purl stitch (p)

1 Hold the needle with the stitches in your left hand, with the loose yarn at the front of the work. Insert the right-hand needle from right to left into the front of the first stitch on the left-hand needle. Wrap the yarn from right to left, up and over the point of the right-hand needle.

Knit stitch (k)

1 Hold the needle with the cast-on stitches in your left hand, with the loose yarn at the back of the work. Insert the right-hand needle from left to right through the front of the first stitch on the left-hand needle. Wrap the yarn from left to right over the point of the right-hand needle.

2 Draw the yarn through the stitch, thus forming a new stitch on the right-hand needle. Slip the original stitch off the left-hand needle. To knit a row, repeat until all the stitches have been transferred from the left-hand needle.

2 Draw the yarn through the stitch, thus forming a new stitch on the right-hand needle. Slip the original stitch off the left-hand needle, keeping the new stitch on the right-hand needle. To purl a row, repeat until all the stitches have been transferred from the left-hand needle to the right-hand needle.

Knit through the back of loop (Ktbl)

Work as for a knit stitch but insert the right-hand needle from left to right through the back of the first stitch on the left-hand needle.

Purl through the back of loop (Ptbl)

Work as a purl stitch but insert the right-hand needle from left to right through the back of the first stitch on the left-hand needle.

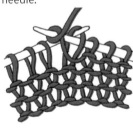

Slip stitch

Following the stitch pattern set, insert the right-hand needle into the first stitch on the left-hand needle as if to knit or purl. Transfer it on to the right-hand needle without wrapping the yarn around the right-hand needle to make a new stitch.

Shaping

This is achieved by increasing or decreasing the number of stitches you are working.

Increasing

The simplest method of increasing one stitch is to create two stitches out of one stitch. Work a stitch into the front of the stitch to be increased into; then, before slipping it off the needle, place the right-hand needle behind the left-hand one and work again into the back of it.

Slip the original stitch off the left-hand needle.

Making a stitch (M1)

Another form of increasing involves working into the strand between two stitches.

1 Insert the right-hand needle from front to back under the horizontal strand that runs between the stitches on the right- and left-hand needles.

2 Insert the left-hand needle under the strand from front to back, twisting it as shown, to prevent a hole from forming, and knit (or purl) through the back of the loop. Slip the new stitch off the left-hand needle.

Decreasing (K2tog, K2togtbl, P2tog, P2togtbl)

The simplest method of decreasing one stitch is to work two stitches together.

To knit two stitches together (k2tog), insert the right-hand needle from left to right through the front of the second stitch and then first stitch nearest the tip of the left-hand needle and knit them together as one stitch.

To knit two together through the back of the loops (k2togtbl), insert the right-hand needle from right to left through the back of the first and then second stitch nearest the tip of the left-hand needle and knit them together as one stitch.

To purl two stitches together (p2tog), insert the right-hand needle from right to left through the front of the first and then second stitch nearest the tip of the left-hand needle, then purl them together as one stitch.

To purl two together through the back of the loops (p2togtbl), insert the right-hand needle from left to right through the back of the second and then first stitch nearest the tip of the needle and purl them together as one stitch.

Casting off

This is the most commonly used method of securing stitches once you have finished a piece of knitting. The cast-off edge should have the same 'give' or elasticity as the fabric, and you should cast off in the stitch used for the main fabric unless the pattern directs otherwise.

Knitwise

Knit two stitches. *Using the point of the left-hand needle, lift the first stitch on the right-hand needle over the second, then drop it off the needle. Knit the next stitch and repeat from * until all stitches have been worked off the left-hand needle and only one stitch remains on the right-hand needle. Cut the yarn, leaving enough to sew in the end, thread the end through the stitch, then slip it off the needle. Draw the yarn up firmly to fasten off.

Purlwise

Work as for knitwise but purl the stitches rather than knit them.

Sewing Tips

Finishing techniques

You may have finished knitting but there is one crucial step still to come, the sewing up of the seams. It is tempting to start this as soon as you cast off the last stitch but a word of caution: make sure that you have good light and plenty of time to complete the task.

Mattress stitch (side edges)

This stitch makes an almost invisible seam on the knit side of stocking stitch. Thread a tapestry needle with yarn and position the pieces side by side, right sides facing.

1 Working from the bottom of the seam to the top, come up from back to front at the base of the seam, to the left of the first stitch in from the edge, on the left-hand side and leave a 10cm (4in) tail of yarn. Take the

needle across to the right-hand piece, to the right of the first stitch, and pass the needle under the first two of the horizontal bars that divide the columns of stitches above the cast-on.

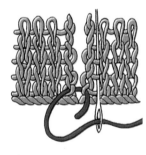

2 Take the needle across to the left-hand piece, insert the needle down where it last emerged on the left-hand edge and pass the needle under two of the horizontal bars that divide the columns of stitches. Take the needle across to the right-hand piece, insert the needle down through the fabric where it last emerged on the right-hand edge and pass the needle under the first two of the

horizontal bars that divide the columns of stitches above the cast-on. Repeat step 2 until the seam has been closed.

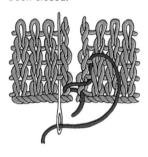

Mattress stitch (top and bottom edges)

Thread a tapestry needle with yarn and position the pieces top and bottom, right sides facing outermost. Working right to left, come up from back to front through the centre of the first stitch on the right edge of the seam. Take the needle to across the top piece, pass the needle under the two loops of the stitch above, then go down again, through the fabric, where the needle emerged on the lower piece. Repeat with the next stitch to the left.

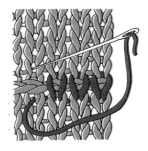

Whip stitch

Thread a tapestry needle with yarn and position the pieces right sides together with the edge to be worked at the top. Working right to left, and always from back to front, pass the needle through the outermost strands of the edge fabric.

Inserting stuffing

As with all soft toys, how you stuff your doll will directly affect the finished appearance.

Stuff firmly, but do not stretch the knitting. Always stuff the extremities, such as the legs and arms, first and mould into shape as you go along. The amount of stuffing needed for each doll depends on the knitting tension and your individual taste.

Adding detail

Embroidery has been used to add detail to the dolls.

Backstitch

Working from right to left, come up slightly to the left of the start of the line of stitching (A), go down at B and then come up at C. Pull the thread through.

Go down again at B to make a backstitch, then come up at D, ready for the next stitch and then continue to create a solid line of short straight stitches.

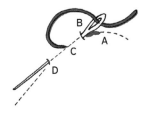

Satin stitch

Work a series of short straight stitches, parallel to each other, to create a pad of stitches.

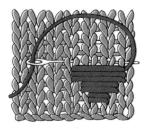

French knots

1 Come up at point A (at which the stitch will sit), wrap the thread twice around the needle in an anticlockwise direction.

2 Push the wraps together and slide to the end of the needle. Go down close to the start point (A), pulling the thread through to form a knot.

Templates

All templates have been reduced to 50% of their size. To enlarge them to the correct size, simply photocopy the pattern using the enlargement button on a photocopier. Photocopy all templates at 200%. You can also find the full-size templates ready to download from www.LoveCrafts.co.uk

Coat (page 28)

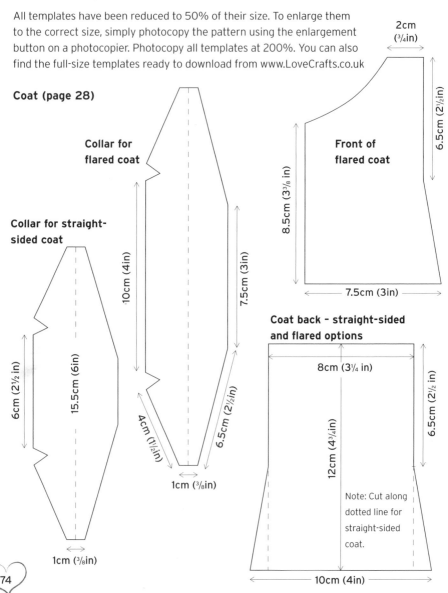

Collar for flared coat

Collar for straight-sided coat

10cm (4in)

15.5cm (6in)

6cm (2½ in)

1cm (⅜in)

7.5cm (3in)

4cm (1½in)

6.5cm (2½in)

1cm (⅜in)

2cm (¾in)

Front of flared coat

8.5cm (3⅜ in)

6.5cm (2½in)

7.5cm (3in)

Coat back – straight-sided and flared options

8cm (3¼ in)

12cm (4¾in)

6.5cm (2½in)

Note: Cut along dotted line for straight-sided coat.

10cm (4in)

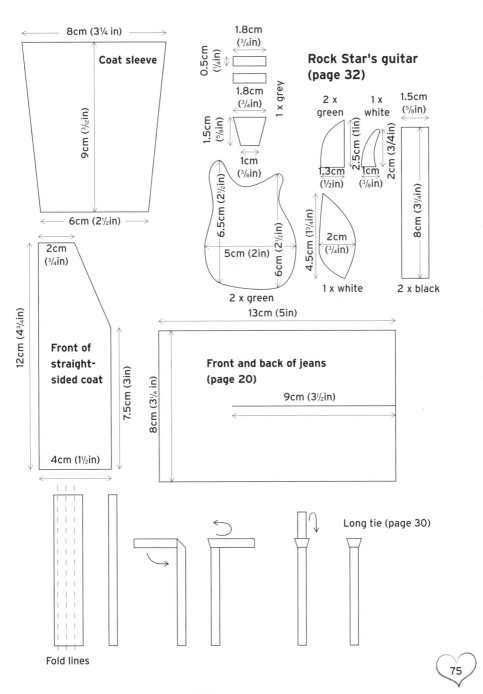

8cm (3¼ in)

Coat sleeve

9cm (3½in)

6cm (2½in)

1.8cm (¾in)

0.5cm (¼in)

1.8cm (¾in)

1 x grey

Rock Star's guitar (page 32)

1.5cm (⅝in)

1cm (⅜in)

2 x green

2.5cm (1in)

1 x white

1cm (⅜in)

2cm (¾in)

1.5cm (⅝in)

1.3cm (½in)

8cm (3¼in)

2 x black

6.5cm (2½in)

5cm (2in)

6cm (2½in)

2 x green

4.5cm (1¾in)

2cm (¾in)

1 x white

12cm (4¾in)

2cm (¾in)

Front of straight-sided coat

7.5cm (3in)

4cm (1½in)

13cm (5in)

Front and back of jeans (page 20)

8cm (3¼ in)

9cm (3½in)

Long tie (page 30)

Fold lines

75

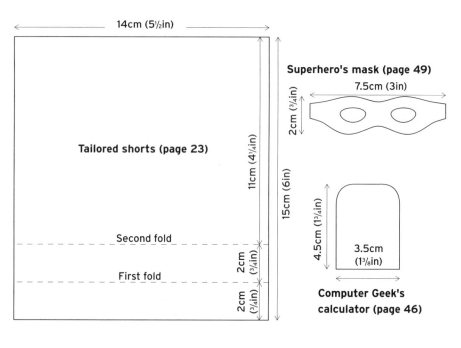

Tailored shorts (page 23)

14cm (5½in)

15cm (6in)

11cm (4¼in)

Second fold

First fold

2cm (¾in)

2cm (¾in)

Superhero's mask (page 49)

7.5cm (3in)

2cm (¾in)

4.5cm (1¾in)

3.5cm (1⅜in)

Computer Geek's calculator (page 46)

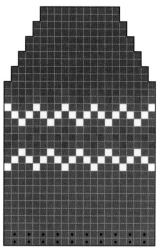

Front and back

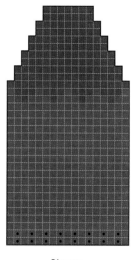

Sleeve

Fair Isle raglan sweater (page 24)

Rowan Pure Wool DK (100% super wash wool; appr 130m/142yds per 50g ball):
  1 ball in 036 Kiss (A)
  1 ball in 013 Enamel (B)
  1 ball in 010 Indigo (C)

Note: Complete neckband us▮ C and instructions on page 2◂

◼ A
☐ B
◼ C
▣ P on RS, K on WS

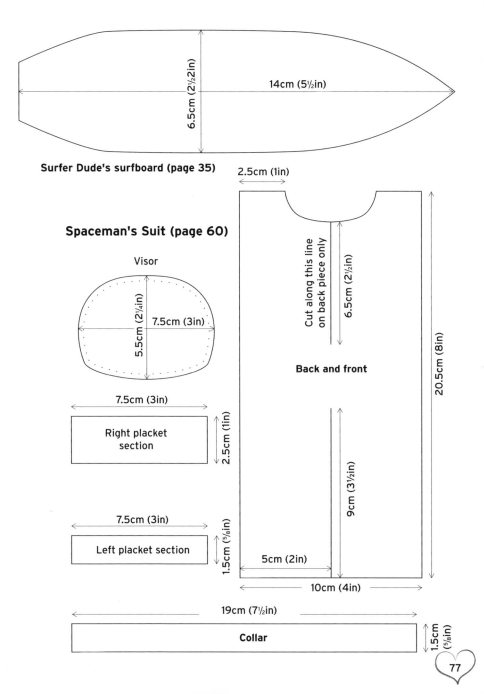

6.5cm (2½2in)

14cm (5½in)

Surfer Dude's surfboard (page 35)

Spaceman's Suit (page 60)

2.5cm (1in)

Cut along this line
on back piece only

6.5cm (2½in)

Visor

5.5cm (2¼in)

7.5cm (3in)

Back and front

20.5cm (8in)

7.5cm (3in)

**Right placket
section**

2.5cm (1in)

9cm (3½in)

7.5cm (3in)

Left placket section

1.5cm (⅝in)

5cm (2in)

10cm (4in)

19cm (7½in)

Collar

1.5cm
(⅝in)

77

Fireman (page 42)

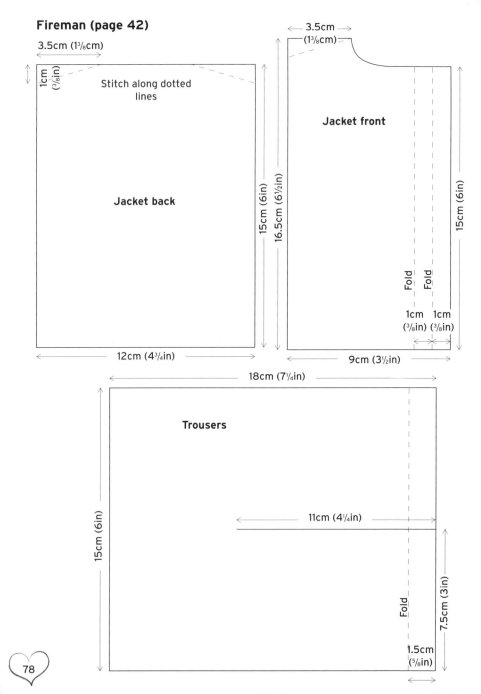

3.5cm (1³⁄₈cm)

1cm (³⁄₈in)

Stitch along dotted lines

Jacket back

15cm (6in)

12cm (4³⁄₄in)

3.5cm (1³⁄₈cm)

Jacket front

16.5cm (6½in)

15cm (6in)

Fold Fold

1cm (³⁄₈in) 1cm (³⁄₈in)

9cm (3½in)

18cm (7¼in)

Trousers

15cm (6in)

11cm (4¼in)

Fold

7.5cm (3in)

1.5cm (⁵⁄₈in)

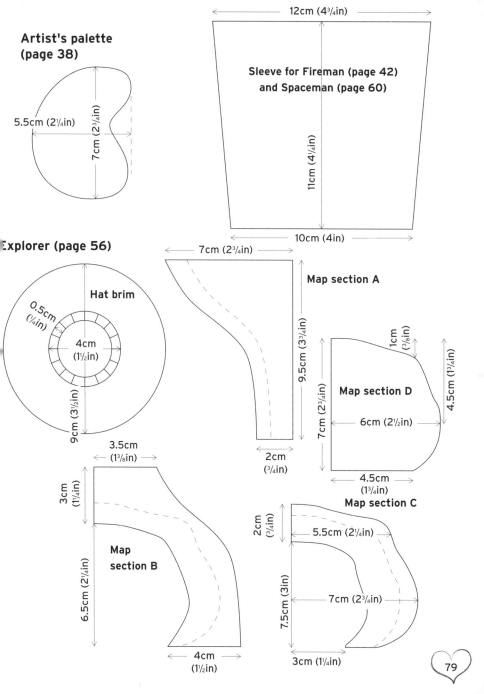

Artist's palette
(page 38)

5.5cm (2¼in)

7cm (2¾in)

12cm (4¾in)

**Sleeve for Fireman (page 42)
and Spaceman (page 60)**

11cm (4¼in)

10cm (4in)

Explorer (page 56)

Hat brim

0.5cm (¼in)

4cm (1½in)

9cm (3½in)

7cm (2¾in)

Map section A

9.5cm (3¾in)

2cm (¾in)

Map section D

1cm (⅜in)

4.5cm (1¾in)

7cm (2¾in)

6cm (2½in)

4.5cm (1¾in)

3.5cm (1⅜in)

3cm (1¼in)

**Map
section B**

6.5cm (2¼in)

4cm (1½in)

Map section C

2cm (¾in)

5.5cm (2¼in)

7.5cm (3in)

7cm (2¾in)

3cm (1¼in)

Abbreviations

approx	approximately
cm	centimetre(s)
g	gram(s)
in	inch(es)
k	knit
k2tog	knit two stitches (or number stated) together
k2togtbl	knit two stitches (or number stated) together through back of loops
LH	left hand
m	metre(s)
m1	make one stitch
mm	millimetre(s)
oz	ounce(s)
p	purl
p2sso	pass two (or number stated) slipped stitches over
p2tog	purl two stitches (or number stated) together
p2togtbl	purl two stitches (or number stated) together through back of loops
psso	pass slipped stitch over
RH	right hand
RS	right side
st(s)	stitch(es)
tbl	through back of loop
tog	together
WS	wrong side
yd(s)	yard(s)
[ ]	work directions within square brackets as directed

First published in the United Kingdom in 2014 by
Collins & Brown
10 Southcombe Street
London
W14 0RA

An imprint of Anova Books Company Ltd

ISBN 978-1-90939-738-5

A CIP catalogue record for this book is available from the British Library.

10 9 8 7 6 5 4 3 2 1

Photography by Rachel Whiting

Reproduction by Mission Productions Ltd, Hong Kong
Printed and bound by 1010 Printing International Ltd, China

This book can be ordered direct from the publisher at www.anovabooks.com

Join our crafting community at LoveCrafts
we look forward to meeting you!